Henry Cuyler Bunner

Rowen

Second Crop

Henry Cuyler Bunner

Rowen
Second Crop

ISBN/EAN: 9783744772501

Printed in Europe, USA, Canada, Australia, Japan

Cover: Foto ©Thomas Meinert / pixelio.de

More available books at **www.hansebooks.com**

ROWEN

"SECOND CROP" SONGS

H. C. BUNNER

> *A Book of Verses underneath the Bough,*
> *A Jug of Wine, a Loaf of Bread, and Thou*
> *Beside me singing in the Wilderness—*
> *Oh, Wilderness were Paradise enow!*
> — *Omar Khayyám*

NEW YORK
CHARLES SCRIBNER'S SONS
1892

Copyright, 1892, by Charles Scribner's Sons

THE DE VINNE PRESS.

TO A. L. B.

I put your rose within our baby's hand,
To bear back with him into Baby-land;
Your rose, you grew it — O my ever dear,
What roses you have grown me, year by year!
Your lover finds no path too hard to go
While your love's roses round about him blow.

   October, 1892.

CONTENTS

	PAGE
AT THE CENTENNIAL BALL — 1889	5
THE LAST OF THE NEW-YEAR'S CALLERS	17
MAY-BLOOM	19
THE LINNET	21
HEAVE HO!	22
AN OLD-FASHIONED LOVE-SONG	24
A LOOK BACK	26
PRUDENCE, SPINNING	28
THE LIGHT	30
GRANT	33
"LET US HAVE PEACE"	36
THE BATTLE OF APIA BAY	38
WILHELM I., EMPEROR OF GERMANY	40
GENERAL SHERMAN	44
LEOPOLD DAMROSCH	47
J. B.	48
MY SHAKSPERE	51
ON SEEING MAURICE LELOIR'S ILLUSTRATIONS TO STERNE'S "SENTIMENTAL JOURNEY"	54

CONTENTS

	PAGE
To a Reader of the XXIst Century	55
For an Old Poet	59
Wilkie Collins	60
For C. J. T. concerning A. D.	62
Edmund Clarence Stedman	63
An Epistle	64
On Reading Certain Published Letters of W. M. T.	67
Chakey Einstein	71
A Fable for Rulers	77
Bismarck Soliloquizes	78
Imitation	82
"Magdalena"	83
"One, Two, Three!"	89
The Little Shop	92
Grandfather Watts's Private Fourth	95
To My Daughter	98
Schubert's Kinder-Scenen	100

ROWEN

WHY do I love New York, my dear?
 I know not. Were my father here —
And his —— and HIS —— the three and I
Might, perhaps, make you some reply.

AT THE CENTENNIAL BALL — 1889

AN OLD MAN'S OLD FANCIES

THERE 'S the music — go, my sweet,
    I will sit and watch you here;
There 's a tingling in my feet
    I 've not felt this many a year.
    But my music 's done, my dear —
'T is enough this heart can beat
    Time to strains that stir your heart;
'T is enough these eyes can see
    Fresh young fires of pleasure start
In the eyes you turn to me.
    Loving, yet, my dear,
    Loath to linger here —
Music-maddened, all impatient to be free.

ROWEN

Go, the music swells and rises — go!
    Younger faces wait you where
    All a-tremble is the air,
And a rhythmic murmur low
    Wavers to and fro —
Life and dance and clasp of lover's hands await you there.
Go, my child, with cheeks that burn,
    Eyes that shine, and fluttering breast,
Go, and leave me — not alone!
    In the dance you shall be prest
Close, and all your soul shall turn
    Tender at the music's tone;
        But more close, more tenderly
        Shall the exultant harmony
Speak to this old, awakened heart, that hears
    The voices of dead years.

She goes — and from below, up-springing,
    The stress and swell of lilting sound
Set one vast field of color swinging
    In sinuous measure round and round.
        The fiddle-bows go up in the air,
            And the fiddle-bows go down;
        And the girl of mine with the yellow hair
        Is dancing to an old-time air
            With the maids of New York town.

ROWEN

My eyes grow dim to see;
But the music sends a song to me,
And here's the song that comes from below —
From the dancing tip of the fiddle-bow:

THE BALL — 1789

THE Town is at the Ball to-night,
    The Town is at the Ball;
From the Battery to Hickory Lane
    The Beaux come one and all.
The French folk up along the Sound
    Took carriage for the city,
And Madge the Belle, from New Rochelle,
    Will stop with Lady Kitty.

And if the Beaux could have their way
    Their choice would be, in Brief,
That Madge the Belle should lead the ball
    And open with THE CHIEF.
Though Lady Kitty's high estate
    May give his choice some reason,
By Right Divine Madge holds her place —
    The Toast of all the Season.

ROWEN

Behold her as she trips the floor
  By Lady Kitty's side —
How low bows Merit at her glance,
  And Valor, true and tried!
Each hand that late the sword-hilt grasped
  Would fain her hand be pressing —
But, ah! fair Madge, who'll wear your badge
  Is past all wooer's guessing.

The Colonel bows his powdered head
  Well nigh unto her feet;
Fame's Trump rings dull unto his ears,
  That wait her Accents sweet.
The young Leftenant, Trig and Trim,
  Who lately won his spurs,
Casts love-sick glances in her way,
  And wins no glance of hers.

Before her bows the Admiral,
  Whose head was never bowed
Before the foamy-crested wave
  That wet the straining shroud.
And all his pretty midshipmen,
  They stand there in a line,
Saluting this Fair Craft that sails
  With no surrendering sign.

ROWEN

And so she trips across the floor
  On Lady Kitty's arm,
And grizzled pates and frizzled pates
  All bow before her charm.
And she will dance the minuet,
  A-facing Lady Kitty,
Nor miss THE CHIEF — she hath, in brief,
  Her choice of all the city.

*   *   *   *   *   *

But in the minuet a hand
  Shall touch her finger-tips,
And almost to a Kiss shall turn
  The Smile upon her lips;
And he is but a midship boy,
  And she is Madge the Belle;
But never to Chief nor to Admiral
  Such a tale her lips shall tell.

*   *   *   *   *   *

The Town is at the Ball to-night,
  The Town is at the Ball,
And the Town shall talk as never before
  Ere another night shall fall;
And men shall rave in Rector street,
  And men shall swear in Pine,
And hearts shall break for Madge's sake
  From Bay to City Line.

ROWEN

And Lady Kit shall wring her hands,
   And write the tale to tell
(To that much dreaded Maiden Aunt
   Who lives at New Rochelle)
All of a gallant Midshipman
   Who wooed in April weather
The Fairest of All at the Chieftain's Ball —
   And they ran away together!

And from below the music flowing
   Has taken a measured, mocking fall,
And forward, backward, coming, going,
   They dance the Minuet of the Ball.
And even as once her grandmama
   Went flitting to and fro
In a dance she danced with grandpapa
   One hundred years ago—
     So, while the fiddle-bows go up,
       And the fiddle-bows go down,
     A daughter of mine with yellow hair
     Is dancing to an old-time air
       With the maids of New York town.

And now again, in cadence changing,
   The music takes a waltzing swing,
And sets an old man's fancies ranging
   Among the tunes his memories sing: —

ROWEN

I hear a sound of strings long slackened,
    The hum of many a stringless bow
On fiddles broken, warped and blackened
    With dust of years of long ago;
And hear the waltz that thrilled and quivered
    Along the yearning pulse of youth,
And unto two dumb hearts delivered
    The message of Love's hidden truth.

THE BALL — 1861

To the front at morn!
    To the front at the break of day!
And the transport ship lies tossing on the waves of the lower bay.

    Her sails are white
In the silver stream of the moon;
The moon will soon be red as blood, her sails will be reddened soon.

    To us who go
Is given a dance to-night —
We may clasp our arms around women and gather the strength to fight.

ROWEN

    Clasp Heaven so close!
Look in Love's eyes and part!
Will the bullet that kills the body make an end of the
    hunger of heart?

    To our breasts they strain,
Beautiful, warm with life —
Make men of us who would make us heroes for mortal
    strife.

    Can I hold you thus,
And release you, all unsaid?
Know I shall want you, dead or living, and dream you
    may want me, dead?

    The last, last dance —
For the gray of the morn is near —
Cling to me once, till I learn the tune that shall out-
    sing Death at my ear!

    Cling to me once, but once —
This is my whole life's round!
Give me to face Death's silence this moment of motion
    and sound.

    *   *   *   *   *   *

ROWEN

Then, as the word unsaid
Found voice in the music's tone,
She looked in my face, and I knew that my soul should
    not go alone.

And the gray dawn came,
But to us had come a light
To make the face of Life and the face of Death shine
    bright.

   *   *   *   *   *   *

To the front at morn!
To the front at the break of day!
Farewell, I said, my Love, and love went with me upon
    my way.

So, through the weary years
Of prayers and tears
  She waited for me, till I came at last;
Came when the soldier's work was done,
And the one holy end of war was won,
  And parting-time was past.

And once again the old tune, winging
  Its way to hearts that still were young,
Set brain and pulse and spirit swinging,
  And once again to me she clung.

ROWEN

And then — but, ah! my music's done —
   For this short way I have to go
An old tune in my mind may run
   That she and I once used to know,
And make an old man's memories stir —
   But all earth's music died with her.
But for you below, my sweet —
   You she left me — still for you
Bowstrings quiver, batons beat,
   And the fiddles thrill you through.
Yours it is to dance, and still,
   Dancing, you may look in eyes
Quick to love you, if you will —
   Quick to turn to high emprise
When the land that gave them birth
Makes the test of manhood's worth.

But, for me, my music's done, —
   I can only sit and hear
Through your whirl of tunes the one
   That Love holds dear.

While the fiddle-bows go up in the air,
   And the fiddle-bows go down,
And the girl of mine with the yellow hair
Is dancing to an old-time air
   With the maids of New York town.

THERE'S but one thing to sing about,
    And poor's the song that does without;
And many a song would not live long
Were it not for the theme that is never worked out.

THE LAST OF THE NEW YEAR'S CALLERS

THE STORY OF AN OLD MAN, AN OLD MAN'S FRIENDSHIP, AND A NEW CARD-BASKET

THE door is shut — I think the fine old face
    Trembles a little, round the under lip;
His look is wistful — can it be the place
    Where, at his knock, the bolt was quick to slip
(It had a knocker then), when, bravely decked,
    He took, of New Year's, with his lowest bow,
His glass of egg-nog, white and nutmeg-flecked,
    From her who is — where is the young bride now?

O Greenwood, answer! Through your ample gate
    There went a hearse, these many years ago;
And often by a grave — more oft of late —
    Stands an old gentleman, with hair like snow.
Two graves he stands by, truly; for the friend
    Who won her, long has lain beside his wife;
And their old comrade, waiting for the end,
    Remembers what they were to him in life.

ROWEN

And now he stands before the old-time door,
  A little gladdened in his lonely heart
To give of love for those that are no more
  To those that live to-day a generous part.
Ay, *She* has gone, sweet, loyal, brave and gay —
  But then, her daughter's grown and wed the while;
And the old custom lingers: New Year's Day,
  Will not she greet him with her mother's smile?

But things are changed, ah, changed, you see;
We keep no New Year's, now, not we —
        It's an old-time day,
        And an old-time way,
And an old-time fashion we've chosen to cut —
        And the dear old man
        May wait as he can
In front of the old-time door that's *shut*.

MAY-BLOOM

OH, for you that I never knew! —
    Now that the Spring is swelling,
And over the way is a whitening may,
    In the yard of my neighbor's dwelling.

O may, oho! Do your sisters blow
    Out there in the country grasses,
A-mocking the white of the cloudlet light
    That up in the blue sky passes?

Here in town the grass it is brown
    Right under your beautiful clusters;
But your sisters thrive where the sward 's alive
    With emerald lights and lusters.

Dream of my dreams! vision that seems
    Ever to scorn my praying,
Love that I wait, face of my fate,
    Come with me now a-maying.

ROWEN

Soul of my soul ! all my life long,
    Looking for you I wander;
Long have I sought — shall I find naught
    Under the may-bushes yonder?

Oh, for you that I never knew,
    Only in dreams that bind you! —
By Spring's own grace I shall know your face
    When under the may I find you!

THE LINNET

ALL day he sat in silence,
    In his shining cage sat he,
And the day grew dim, but never from him
    Came a note of melody.

But late at night in silence
    Heart to heart came He and She
To the darkened room; and out of the gloom
    Came the linnet's melody.

HEAVE HO!

HEAVE ho! the anchor over the bow,
    And off to sea go I;
The wild wind blows, and nobody knows
    That I have you always nigh.
Right close in my heart I can keep you here
    In memory fond and true,
For there 'll never be one like you, my dear —
    There 'll never be one like you.

Oho! the billows of Biscay Bay,
    And the stars of the southern sea!
But the dark-haired girls may shake their curls,
    With never a look from me;
For the thought of my love shall be ever near,
    Though wide is the ocean blue,
And there 'll never be one like you, my dear —
    There 'll never be one like you.

ROWEN

The end of the world is a weary way,
   And I know not where it lies,
And maidens fair may smile on me there,
   And girls with laughing eyes;
But in all the days of all the year,
   Though I wander the whole world through,
There 'll never be one like you, my dear —
   There 'll never be one like you.

AN OLD-FASHIONED LOVE-SONG

TELL me what within her eyes
  Makes the forgotten Spring arise,
And all the day, if kind she looks,
Flow to a tune like tinkling brooks;
Tell me why, if but her voice
Falls on men's ears, their souls rejoice;
Tell me why, if only she
Doth come into the companie,
All spirits straight enkindled are,
As if a moon lit up a star.

> *Tell me this that 's writ above,*
> *And I will tell you why I love.*

Tell me why the foolish wind
Is to her tresses ever kind,
And only blows them in such wise
As lends her beauty some surprise;

ROWEN

Tell me why no changing year
Can change from Spring, if she appear;
Tell me why to see her face
Begets in all folk else a grace
That makes them fair, as love of her
Did to a gentler nature stir.

Tell me why, if she but go
Alone across the fields of snow,
All fancies of the Springs of old
Within a lover's breast grow bold;
Tell me why, when her he sees,
Within him stirs an April breeze;
And all that in his secret heart
Most sacredly was set apart,
And most was hidden, then awakes,
At the sweet joy her coming makes.

Tell me what is writ above,
And I will tell you why I love.

A LOOK BACK

A CASTLE-YARD—1585

(*Enter* SIR BEVYS, *mounted. There comes to meet him, bearing a cup of wine*, MAID MARGERY.)

WHAT, Madge — nay, Madge! why, sweetheart, is it thou?
Faith, but I knew thee not — nor know thee yet!
Madge — Margery — child — coz, thou 'st grown apace.
Why, what a merry coming home is this!
To have my cousin meet me in the court,
My half-grown cousin, grown an angel half,
Lifting a cup to make the wanderer welcome,
With such an arm — why, Margery, 't was a reed,
A meagre, sun-specked reed, when last I saw it,
Three years ago — coz, these were busy years
That dealt so kindly with thee. I set forth
Three years agone last Michaelmas, and thou —

ROWEN

Why, thou and Rupert were an elfish pair
Of freckled striplings — yea, thy elbows, Madge,
My cousin Margery, were as rasping sharp
As old Dame Ursula her tongue — ay, cousin,
I 'll drink once more, so thou wilt lift the cup
And show that snowy round again. And Rupert,
My brother Rupert, how fares he? Nay, nay!
First in the tourney? Sturdiest Knight of all?
Gad's grace, the world has wagged while I have wandered.
I 'll tell thee this, thou Hebe hazel-eyed,
Had I seen further I had wandered less.
But who 'd have thought the slender girl I left,
The straggling weed — thy present grace may pardon
My memory rude — had grown to this fair flower —
To this bright comeliness, this young perfection,
This — this —
   Maid Margery let her lashes down,
And bent her head — perhaps the sunset fell
A trifle 'thwart her face — perhaps she blushed,
As, looking down into the empty cup,
She answered very softly:
     "Rupert did."

PRUDENCE, SPINNING

A STUDIO STUDY

I.

PRUDENCE, sitting by the fire,
Lift your head a little higher —
How the firelight ripples in
And out the dimple of your chin —
How your sidewise-tilted head
Snares the flickering gleams of red;
Snares them in a golden net
Than your distaff fleecier yet!
O my Prudence, turn — but no —
Shall a century backward flow?
Prudence — ah, awelladay!
You 're a hundred years away.

ROWEN

II.

He who looks upon you hears
Through a hundred bygone years
Whir of wheel and foot's light tap
On the treadle, and the snap
Of the rose-red hickory logs,
Sputtering, sinking on the dogs;
And your breath he almost feels
In a gentle sigh that steals
From your lips, while hand in head
Weave a dream and spin a thread—
Prudence—who 'd believe it, pray?
You 're a hundred years away.

* * * *

Silent was the studio,
Duller grew the hickory's glow,
And the skylight, cold and faint,
Seemed to frown—"'T is late to paint!"
Prudence drooped a weary head,
Hearing not the painter's tread,
As he crossed the room and bent
Just where blush and firelight blent.
O my Prudence, model fair!
Where 's your prim provincial air?
Prudence—ah, awelladay!
How a century slips away!

THE LIGHT

THERE is no shadow where my love is laid;
  For (ever thus I fancy in my dream,
  That wakes with me and wakes my sleep) some gleam
Of sunlight, thrusting through the poplar shade,
Falls there; and even when the wind has played
  His requiem for the Day, one stray sunbeam,
  Pale as the palest moonlight glimmers seem,
Keeps sentinel for Her till starlights fade.

And I, remaining here and waiting long,
  And all enfolded in my sorrow's night,
    Who not on earth again her face may see,—
For even memory does her likeness wrong,—
  Am blind and hopeless, only for this light —
    This light, this light, through all the years to be.

WHICH was the harder to lay down,
    Art and ambition, or a crown?
The sceptre or the fiddle-bow?
I know not. All were loath to go.
Yet who would call, did Fate permit,
One of these back to what he quit?

GRANT

SMILE on, thou new-come Spring — if on thy breeze
The breath of a great man go wavering up
And out of this world's knowledge, it is well.

Kindle with thy green flame the stricken trees,
And fire the rose's many-petaled cup,
Let bough and branch with quickening life-blood swell—
But Death shall touch his spirit with a life
That knows not years or seasons. Oh, how small
Thy little hour of bloom! Thy leaves shall fall,
And be the sport of winter winds at strife;
But he has taken on eternity.
Yea, of how much this Death doth set him free! —
Now are we one to love him, once again.
The tie that bound him to our bitterest pain
Draws him more close to Love and Memory.

ROWEN

O Spring, with all thy sweetheart frolics, say,
   Hast thou remembrance of those earlier springs
When we wept answer to the laughing day,
   And turned aside from green and gracious things?
There was a sound of weeping over all —
   Mothers uncomforted, for their sons were not;
   And there was crueler silence: tears grew hot
In the true eyes that would not let them fall.
Up from the South came a great wave of sorrow
   That drowned our hearthstones, splashed with blood
      our sills;
To-day, that spared, made terrible To-morrow
   With thick presentiment of coming ills.
Only we knew the Right — but oh, how strong,
How pitiless, how insatiable the Wrong!

And then the quivering sword-hilt found a hand
That knew not how to falter or grow weak;
And we looked on, from end to end the land,
And felt the heart spring up, and rise afresh
The blood of courage to the whitened cheek,
And fire of battle thrill the numbing flesh.
Ay, there was death, and pain, and dear ones missed,
And lips forever to grow pale unkissed;
But lo, the man was here, and this was he;
And at his hands Faith gave us victory.

ROWEN

Spring, thy poor life, that mocks his body's death,
Is but a candle's flame, a flower's breath.
He lives in days that suffering made dear
Beyond all garnered beauty of the year.
He lives in all of us that shall outlive
The sensuous things that paltry time can give.
This Spring the spirit of his broken age
   Across the threshold of its anguish stole —
All of him that was noble, fearless, sage,
   Lives in his lovèd nation's strengthened soul.

"LET US HAVE PEACE"

U. S. GRANT — JULY 23, 1885

HIS name was as a sword and shield,
    His words were armèd men,
He mowed his foemen as a field
    Of wheat is mowed — and then
Set his strong hand to make the shorn earth smile again.

Not in the whirlwind of his fight,
    The unbroken line of war,
Did he best battle for the right —
    His victory was more:
Peace was his triumph, greater far than all before.

Who in the spirit and love of peace
    Takes sadly up the blade,
Makes war on war, that wars may cease —
    He striveth undismayed,
And in the eternal strength his mortal strength is stayed.

ROWEN

    Peace, that he conquered for our sake —
        This is his honor, dead.
    We saw the clouds of battle break
        To glory o'er his head —
But brighter shone the light about his dying bed.

    Dead is thy warrior, King of Life,
        Take thou his spirit flown;
    The prayer of them that knew his strife
        Goes upward to thy throne —
Peace be to him who fought — and fought for Peace alone.

THE BATTLE OF APIA BAY

MARCH 15, 1889

THE portholes black look over the bay
   To the ports on the other side;
And the gun in each grim square porthole dim
   Is guarding a nation's pride.

Two fleets are they in an alien sea,
   And whether as friends or foes,
Till the diplomats' prattle decides their battle,
   Nor sailor nor captain knows.

But strange to each is the sun that starts
   The pitch in the white deck's seams,
While the watch, half dozing with eyes half closing,
   Go home in their waking dreams.

And strange is the land that lies about,
   And the folk with faces brown,
To the Pommerland boy with the yellow beard,
   And the boy from Portland town.

ROWEN

And each looks over the bay to each —
  Is the end of it peace or war?
And the wish that's best in each brave young breast
  Is the wish for a run ashore.

* * * * *

Death came out of the sea last night —
  Death is aboard this morn —
The water is over the war-ship's prow,
  And her snow-white sails are torn.

And the bright blue waves that leap to catch
  The glint of the tropic sun
Roll overhead, and beneath are the dead,
  For the battle is fought and won.

There's the Pommerland boy with his yellow beard,
  And the Maine boy bearded brown;
And there's weeping sore on the Pommerland shore;
  There are tears in Portland town.

O ships that guard two nations' pride,
  Death had no need for ye!
They went to their fate through no man's hate —
  Death's servant was the Sea.

WILHELM I., EMPEROR OF GERMANY

March 22, 1797 — January 2, 1861 — January 18, 1871 — March 9, 1888

WHEN the gray Emperor at the Gates of Death
    Stood silent, up from Earth there came the sound
Of mourning and dismay; man's futile breath
    Vexed the still air around.

But silent stood the Emperor and alone
Before the ever silent gates of stone
    That open and close at either end of life;
As who, having fought his fight,
Stands, overtaken of night,
    And hears afar the receding sound of strife.

ROWEN

Wide open swing the gates:

> *Hail, Hohenzollern, hail to thee!*
> *If thou be he*
> *For whom each hero waits,*
> *Hail, hail to thee!*

So rings
The chorus of the Kings.
This is the House of Death, the Hall of Fame,
Lit, its vast length, by torches' flickering flame;
And, with their faces by the torch-fires lit,
Around the board the expectant monarchs sit.
Filled are their drink-horns with the immortals' wine —
They wait for him, the latest of their line.

> Under the flags they sit, beneath
> The which the keen sword spurned its sheath.
> Under the flags that first were woven
>   To bring the fire to stranger eyes;
> That now, at cost of corselets cloven,
>   In lines of tattered trophies rise.
> To greet the newly come they wait —
> The heroes of the German State:

ROWEN

His father, unto whom the west wind blew
The echo of the guns of Waterloo:
That greater FREDERICK, with the lust of power
    Still smoldering in his eyes, his troubled heart
Impatient with the briefness of his hour
    That altered Europe's chart:
And he, the Great Elector, he who first
    Sounded to Poland's King a nation's word:

And he who, earlier, by Rome accursed,
    The trumpet-tone of Martin Luther heard —
        So the long line of faces grim
        Grows faint and dim,
And at the farther end, where lights burn low,
    Where, through a misty glow,
Heroes of German song and story rise
    Gods to our eyes,
Great HERMANN rises, father of a race,
To give the Emperor his place.

  "Come to the table's head,
    Among the ennobled dead!"
He cries: "Nor none shall ask me of thy right."
    Then speaks he to the board:
  "Bow down, in one accord,
To him whose strength is Majesty, not Might.

ROWEN

"Emperor and King he comes; his people's cry
    Pierces our distant sky;
Emperor and King he comes, whose mighty hand
Gathered in one the kingdoms of the land.
    Yet greater far the tale shall be
    That gains him immortality:
To his high task no selfish thought,
No coward hesitance he brought;
All that it was to be a King
    He was, nor counted of the cost.
He rounds our circle — Time may bring
The day when Earth shall need no King —
    All that Kings were, in him Earth lost."

"*Hail, Hohenzollern, hail!*" cried the heroes dead;
And the gray Emperor sat at the table's head.

GENERAL SHERMAN

FEBRUARY 14, 1891

BOWED banners and the drums' thick muffled beat
   For him, and silent crowds along the street;
The stripes of white and crimson on his breast,
And all the trapping of a warrior's rest;
For him the wail of dirges, and the tread
Of the vast army following its dead
Unto the great surrender; half-mast high
For him the flags shall brave the winter sky —
These be his honors: and some old eyes dim
For love's sake, more than fame's — for him, for him!

These things are his; yet not to him alone
Is this proud wealth of ordered honor shown.
Thus to their graves may go all men who stand
Between their country and the foeman's brand:

ROWEN

This is the meed of hardihood in fight,
The formal tribute to a hero's might.
A myriad dead have won the like award—
The unknown, unnumbered servants of the sword.
Hath he no greater honor?

                          Yes, although
It win for his dead clay no funeral show,
Nor none shall tell upon the market-place
What gave this hero his most special grace,
That for his memory, in the years to come,
Shall speak more loud than voice of gun or drum.
Great was his soul in fight. But you and I,
Friend, if need be, can set a face to die.
This land of ours has lovers now as then,
Nor shall time coming find her poor in men,
While the strong blood of our old Saxon strain
Fires at the sound of war in pulse and vein.

But this great warrior was in Peace more great,
More noble in his fealty to the state,
More fine in service, in a subtler way
Meeting the vital duty of the day;
Patient and calm, too simply proud to strive
To keep the glory of his past alive.

So burns it still, and shall burn. Every year
Of that high service made him but more dear,
More trusted, more revered. No lust of power
Led him to lengthen out the battle hour;
He sought no office; he would learn no art
To serve him at the polls or in the mart;
And yet he loved the people, nor did pride
Lead him from common joys and cares aside.
His kindly, homely, grizzled face looked down
On all the merrymaking of the town —
A face that we shall miss: we all were proud
When the Old General smiled upon the crowd.
So lived, so died he. Has a great man passed
And left a life more whole unto the last?

Upon the soldier's coffin let this wreath
Tell of his greatest greatness, sword-in-sheath.

LEOPOLD DAMROSCH

February 15, 1885

WAKED at the waving of thy hand, so near
    Came music to the language of the soul —
Not viol alone, or flute: an ordered whole,
That with one voice spoke to us, subtly clear —
So near it came to all that life holds dear,
    So full it was of messages that stole
    Silently to the spirit — of the roll
Of thunders that the heart leaped up to hear —
That we, who look upon the fallen hand
    That shall not rise for music's sake again
        Upon this earth — we, lingering, well may deem
Thee glad with a great joy, to understand,
    At last, the full and all-revealing strain
        That tells what earthly music may but dream.

J. B.

June 7, 1880.

THE Actor's dead, and memory alone
   Recalls the genial magic of his tone;
Marble nor canvas nor the printed page
Shall tell his genius to another age:
A memory, doomed to dwindle less and less,
His world-wide fame shrinks to this littleness.
Yet if, a half a century from to-day,
A tender smile about our old lips play,
And if our grandchild query whence it came,
We'll say: "A thought of Brougham."—
                          And that is Fame!

I SERVE with love a goodly craft,
　　And proud thereat am I;
And, if I do but work aright,
　　Shall never wholly die.

MY SHAKSPERE

WITH beveled binding, with uncut edge,
    With broad white margin and gilded top,
Fit for my library's choicest ledge,
    Fresh from the bindery, smelling of shop,
In tinted cloth, with a strange design —
    Buskin and scroll-work and mask and crown,
    And an arabesque legend tumbling down —
"The Works of Shakspere" were never so fine.
Fresh from the shop! I turn the page —
    Its "ample margin" is wide and fair,
    Its type is chosen with daintiest care;
    There's a "New French Elzevir" strutting there
That would shame its prototypic age.
Fresh from the shop! O Shakspere mine,
I've half a notion you're much too fine!

There's an ancient volume that I recall,
    In foxy leather much chafed and worn;
Its back is broken by many a fall,
    The stitches are loose and the leaves are torn;

ROWEN

And gone is the bastard title, next
    To the title-page scribbled with owners' names,
    That in straggling old-style type proclaims
That the work is from the corrected text
    Left by the late Geo. Steevens, Esquire.

    The broad sky burns like a great blue fire,
And the Lake shines blue as shimmering steel,
    And it cuts the horizon like a blade;
    And behind the poplar 's a strip of shade —
    The great tall Lombardy on the lawn.
And, lying there in the grass, I feel
    The wind that blows from the Canada shore,
    And in cool, sweet puffs comes stealing o'er,
    Fresh as any October dawn.

I lie on my breast in the grass, my feet
    Lifted boy-fashion, and swinging free,
    The old brown Shakspere in front of me.
And big are my eyes, and my heart 's a-beat;
And my whole soul 's lost — in what? — who knows?
Perdita's charms or Perdita's woes —
Perdita fairy-like, fair and sweet.
    Is any one jealous, I wonder, now,
    Of my love for Perdita? For I vow
    I loved her well. And who can say
    That life would be quite the same life to-day —

ROWEN

That Love would mean so much, if she
Had not taught me its A B C?

The Grandmother, thin and bent and old,
    But her hair still dark and her eyes still bright,
        Totters around among the flowers —
Old-fashioned flowers of pink and white;
And turns with a trowel the dark rich mold
    That feeds the blooms of her heart's delight.
        Ah me! for her and for me the hours
Go by, and for her the smell of earth —
And for me the breeze and a far love's birth,
    And the sun and the sky and all the things
    That a boy's heart hopes and a poet sings.

Fresh from the shop! O Shakspere mine,
It was n't the binding made you divine!
I knew you first in a foxy brown,
In the old, old home, where I laid me down,
    In the idle summer afternoons,
With you alone in the odorous grass,
    And set your thoughts to the wind's low tunes,
And saw your children rise up and pass —
And dreamed and dreamed of the things to be,
Known only, I think, to you and me.

I 've hardly a heart for you dressed so fine —
Fresh from the shop, O Shakspere mine!

ON SEEING MAURICE LELOIR'S ILLUSTRATIONS TO STERNE'S "SENTIMENTAL JOURNEY"

LELOIR, what kinship lies between you two —
This century-vanished Englishman and you? —
You who can lead us, grateful in surprise,
All that he saw to see with trusting eyes —
Nay, at your beck his head peeps, gaunt and hoar,
Out of the window in the po'chaise door.

Is it not this: birth made him of your race
(Though Clonmel and not Calais were the place,)
If heart and fancy be the best of birth?

Some day, Leloir, your spirit, freed from earth,
Walking that special heaven set apart
For those who made religion of their art,
Will meet this elder friend, and he will turn
And speak to you in French — this Laurence Sterne.

TO A READER OF THE XXIst CENTURY

YOU, when you read this book, shall find
How You or We have fallen behind.
Where'er you be, I know you not;
But, if my memory be forgot,
Remember, proud of life and thought
Though *You* may strut, *I* hold you naught.
You *are* not yet — you *may be* — still,
How do I know you ever *will?*

But yet I hope, in future days,
You may exist, to cast your gaze
Round some old bibliomaniac's room,
Shrouded in sober russet gloom,
And let it fall upon this book;
Then turn this page — I'll catch your look.

Aye! though the while this line you read
A coverlet of daisy brede
Shall lie my old-time bed above
And all that was my life and love;

ROWEN

I speak to you from out a day
When *I*, not *You*, can see the Play,
And find the stage's mimicry
More real than are *You* to *Me*.
When blood went slipping through this heart,
I saw it all — I was a part.

This is our day — you turn the page,
And see the pictures of our age.
"A treasure!" cries your bibliopole,
With fervor in his musty soul:
"A Daly private print — a chaste
Example of our fathers' taste.
They made books *then* — who can, in our
Degenerate days of — magnet — power?
See — Ada Rehan, Fisher, Drew,
Dame Gilbert, Lewis — through and through
The sharp-cut plates are clear as new!"
Then comes the old, the tardy praise —
"Those were the drama's palmy days."

But We? You'll see the shadow — now
To us these living creatures bow,
For us they smile — for us they feign
Or love or hatred, joy or pain;
For us this white breast heaves — this voice
Makes hearts too young too much rejoice;

ROWEN.

For us those splendid eyes are lit;
For us awakes embodied wit;
For us the music and the light —
The listening faces, flushed and bright;
The glow, the passion, and the dream —
To you — how far it all must seem!

You know the names — but we behold,
In sweet old age that is not old,
Though Time play tricks with face and hair,
Our Gentlewoman past compare.
We see her deftly thread the set
Old figures of the minuet;
We see her Partner's snow-crowned face
Bent o'er her hand in antique grace.

You know the names — before our eyes
Proud Katherine's anger flames and dies;
For us Petruchio pays his court;
For us the high tempestuous port,
Lowered at last in humble, sweet
Submission at a husband's feet.
You know the names — but ah! who hears
The laughter when one face appears?

You know the names — but what are they?
We know the folk that make the Play!

ROWEN.

Love's merry Up, Love's doleful Down,
The fickle fashion of the town
Take form and shape for us, and show
To heart and eye the world we know.

You have the pictures, and the names
That are but Yours as they are Fame's;
See them, O dim Potential Shade,
Even as we see them now arrayed:
Try to put nature's vital hue
Into the faces that you view;
And think, while Fancy labors thus,
This all is breathing Life to Us.

FOR AN OLD POET

WHEN he is old and past all singing,
    Grant, kindly Time, that he may hear
The rhythm through joyous Nature ringing,
    Uncaught by any duller ear.

Grant that, in memory's deeps still cherished,
    Once more may murmur low to him
The winds that sung in years long perished,
    Lit by the suns of days grown dim.

Grant that the hours when first he listened
    To bird-songs manhood may not know,
In fields whose dew for lovers glistened,
    May come back to him ere he go.

Grant only this, O Time most kindly,
    That he may hear the song you sung
When love was new — and, harkening blindly,
    Feign his o'er-wearied spirit young.

With sound of rivers singing round him,
    On waves that long since flowed away,
Oh, leave him, Time, where first Love found him,
    Dreaming To-morrow in To-day!

WILKIE COLLINS

September 23, 1889

WHEN Arabs sat around
    And heard the Thousand Nights —
Beyond the tent's close bound,
    Beyond the watch-fire lights —
Their believing spirits flew
    To a land where strange things seem
As simple things and true,
    And the best truth is a dream.

And when the tale was told —
    Genie and Princess fair
Brought to an end — their gold
    They sought, with an absent air;
And dropped it at His feet
    Who had led to the land of Delight;
And, dreaming of Princesses sweet,
    They passed out into the night.

ROWEN

So, still under your spell,
    Teller of magic tales,
These lines I would fain let tell
    The debt whose payment fails.
Take them: if they were gold
    'T would but discharge a due —
And, for the tales you told,
    I shall remember you.

FOR C. J. T., CONCERNING A. D

HERE shall you see the sweetest mind
That loves our simpler humankind:
The things that touch your heart and mine
He knows by sympathy so fine
That he, an alien, over sea,
Partner in our best thought can be.
Not the ATLANTIC'S swell and moan
Can part his fancy from our own.

    *   *   *   *

See but a child with wistful eyes
THE DOCTOR'S gloomy windows rise,
And that sad comedy is played
That makes us love one little maid:
See the kind face we children knew,
And PRUDENCE is our "Aunty," too;
Think of the madcap loves of youth,
And think of BELL, LOUISE, and RUTH:
Think of the loves not Love, alas!
And of ROSINE in Mont Parnasse:
Dream of the things most sweet and true
That your best moments bring to you,
And find this gentle Poet's art
Voices the thought that stirred your heart.

EDMUND CLARENCE STEDMAN

THOUGH to his song the reeds respondent rustle
    That cradled Pan what time all song was young,
Though in a new world city's restless bustle
    He sounds a lyre in fields Sicilian strung;
Though his the power the days of old to waken,
    Though Nature's melody 's as clear to him
As ere of dryads were the woods forsaken,
    And the fresh world of myth grew faint and dim—
A dearer grace is his when men's eyes glisten
    With closer sympathies his page above,
And near his spirit draws to hearts that listen
    The song that sweetly rounds with Home and Love.

NEW YORK, December 10, 1884.

AN EPISTLE

To Master Brander Matthews, Writer, on the Occasion of his Putting Forth a Book entitled "Pen and Ink"

NEW LONDON, CONN., SEPT. 10, 1888.

Dear Brander:
     I have known thee long, and found
Thee wise in council, and of judgment sound;
Steadfast in friendship, sound and clear in wit,
And more in virtues than may here be writ.
But most I joy, in these machine-made days,
To see thee constant in a craftsman's ways;
That the plain tool that knew thy 'prentice hand
Gathers no rust upon thy writing-stand;
That no Invention saves the labor due
To any Task that 's worth the going through;
That now when butter snubs the stranger churn,
Plain pen and ink still serve a writer's turn.
Though I, more firmly orthodox, still hold,
In dire default of quills, to steel or gold,
And though thy pen be rubber — let it pass —
A breath of blemish on thy soul's clear glass.

ROWEN

There is no "writing fluid" in thy pot,
But honest ink of nutgall brew, God wot!
Thou dost not an electric needle ply,
And, like a housewife with an apple-pie,
Prick thy fair page into a stencil-plate —
Then daub with lampblack for a duplicate.
Nor thine the sloven page whereon the shirk
With the rough tool attempts the finished work,
And introduces to the sight of men
The Valet Pencil for the Master Pen.

Not all like thee, in this uneasy age,
When more by trick than toil we earn our wage!
Here by the sea a gentle poet dwells,
And in fair leisure weaves his magic spells;
And yet doth dare with countenance serene
To weave them on a tinkling steel machine,
Where an impertinent and soulless bell
Rings, at each finished line, a jangling knell.
The muse and I, we love him, and I think
She may forgive his slight to pen and ink,
And let no dull mechanic cam or cog
The lightsome movement of his metres clog;
But oh! I grieve to see his fingers toy
With this base slave in dalliance close and coy,

ROWEN

*While in his standish dries the atrid spring
Where hides the shyer muse that loves to sing.
Give me the old-time ink, black, flowing, free,
And give, oh, give ! the old goose-quill to me —
The goose-quill, whispering of humility.
It whispers to the bard: " Fly not too high !
You flap your wings — remember, so could I.
I cackled in my life-time, it is true ;
But yet again remember, so do You.
And there were some things possible to me
That possible to you will never be.
I stood for hours on one columnar leg,
And, if my sex were such, could lay an egg.
Oh, well for you, if you could thus beget
Material for your morning omelette ;
Or, if things came to such a desperate pass,
You could in calm contentment nibble grass !
Conceited bard ! and can you sink to rest
Upon the feather-pillow of your breast ?"*

*Hold, my dear Brander, to your pot of ink:
The muse sits poised upon that fountain's brink.
And that you long may live to hold a pen
I 'll breathe a prayer ;*
                The world will say " Amen ! "

ON READING CERTAIN PUBLISHED LETTERS OF W. M. T.

IT is as though the gates of heaven swung,
    Once only, backward, and a spirit shone
Upon us, with a face to which there clung
    Naught of that mortal veil which sore belies,
    But looked such love from such high-changèd eyes,
That, even from earth, we knew them for his own.

Knew them for his, and marveled; for he came
    Among us, and went from us, and we knew
Only the smoke and ash that hid the flame,
    Only the cloak and vestment of his soul;
    And knew his priesthood only by his stole —
And, thus unknown, he went his journey through.

Yet there were some who knew him, though his face
    Was never seen by them; although his hand
Lay never warm in theirs, they yet had grace
    To see, past all misjudgment; his true heart
    Throbbed for them in the creatures of his art,
And they could read his words, and understand.

ROWEN

All men may know him now, and know how kind
    The hand in chastisement so sure and strong —
All men may know him now, and dullards blind
    Into the secrets of his soul may see;
    And all shall love — but, Steadfast Greatheart, we,
We knew thee when the wide world did thee wrong.

SAYS the Man in the Moon, "It's a fine world there";
   But he wonders how it can please us
To walk with our heads hanging down in the air —
   For that is the way he sees us.

CHAKEY EINSTEIN

PHARAOH, King of Egypt's land,
    Held you in his cruel hand,
Till the Appointed of the Lord
Led you forth and drowned his horde.
Cushan, Eglon's Moabites,
Jabin, then the Midianites,
Ammonite and Philistine
Held you, by decree divine.
Shishak spoiled you — but the list
Fades in dim tradition's mist —
And on history's page we see
One long tale of misery,
Century after century through —
Chains and lashes for the Jew.
Haman and Antiochus,
Herod, Roman Socius,
Spoiled you, crushed you, various ways,
Till the dawn of Christian days;

ROWEN

Since which time your wrongs and shame
Have remained about the same.
Whipped and chained, your teeth pulled out;
English cat and Russian knout
Made familiar with your back —
When you were n't upon the rack —
Marked for scorn of Christian men;
Pilfered, taxed, and taxed again;
Pilloried, prisoned, burnt and stoned,
Stripped of even the clothes you owned;
Child of Torture, Son of Shame,
Robbed of even a father's name —
In this year of Christian grace,
What's your state and what's your place?
Why you're rich and strong and gay —
Chakey Einstein, owff Browdway!

Myriad signs along the street
Israelitish names repeat.
Lichtenstein and Morgenroth
Sell the pants and sell the coat;
Minzesheimer, Isaacs, Meyer,
Levy, Lehman, Simon, Speyer —
These may just suggest a few
Specimens of Broadway Jew —

ROWEN

And these gentlemen have made
Quite their own the Dry-gootz Trade.
Surely you 're on top to-day,
Chakey Einstein, owff Browdway.

Fat and rich you are, and loud;
Fond of being in a crowd;
Fond of diamonds and rings;
Fond of haberdashers' things;
Fond of color, fond of noise;
Fond of treating "owl der boys"
(Yet, it 's only fair to state,
For yourself, most temperate);
Fond of women, fond of song;
Fond of bad cigars, and strong;
Fond, too much, of Brighton's Race
(Where you 're wholly out of place,
For no Jew in Time's long course
Knew one thing about a horse);
Fond of life, and fond of fun
(Once your "beezness" wholly done);
Open-handed, generous, free,
Full of Christian charity
(Far more full than he who pokes
At your avarice his jokes);

ROWEN

Fond of friends, and ever kind
To the sick and lame and blind
(And, though loud you else may be,
Silent in your charity);
Fond of Mrs. Einstein and
Her too-numerous infant band,
Ever willing they should share
Your enjoyment everywhere —
What of you is left to say,
Chakey Einstein, owff Browdway?

Though you're spurned in some hotels,
You have kin among the swells —
Great musicians, poets true,
Painters, singers not a few,
Own their cousinship to you:
And all England, so they say,
Yearly blooms on Primrose Day
All in memory of a Jew
Of the self-same race as you;
Greatest leader ever known
Since the Queen came to her throne;
Bismarck's only equal foe,
With a thrust for every blow,
One who rose from place to place
To lead the Anglo-Saxon race,

ROWEN

One whose statecraft wise and keen
Made an Empress of a Queen —
You 've your share in Primrose Day,
Chakey Einstein, owff Browdway!

Well, good friend, we look at you
And behold the Conquering Jew:
In despite of all the years
Filled with agonies and fears;
In despite of stake and chain;
In despite of Rome and Spain;
'Spite of prison, rack, and lash,
You are here, and you 've the cash:
You are Trade's uncrownèd king —
You are mostly everything —
Only one small joke, O Jew!
Has the Christian world on you —
When your son, your first-born boy,
Solomon, your fond heart's joy,
Grows to manhood's years, he 'll wed
One a Christian born and bred;
Blue of blood, of lineage old,
Who will take him for his gold —
That 's not all — so far the joke
Is upon the Christian folk.

ROWEN

But, dear Chakey, when he goes
In his proper Sabbath clo'es,
To the House of Worship, he
And his little family,
He will pass the synagogue,
And upon his way will jog
To a Church, wherein his pew
Will bear a name unknown to you —
One quite unknown in old B'nai B'rith —
Eynston maybe — maybe Smith.
That's just as sure as day is day —
Chakey Einstein, owff Browdway!

A FABLE FOR RULERS

(From the French)

A KING of Persia, once upon a day,
  Rode with his courtiers to the chase away.
Thirst o'ertook him in a desert plain,
Where he sought a cooling fount in vain.
Last he chanced upon a garden fine,
Rich in luscious orange, grape, and pine:
"God forbid my thirst I slake!"
Quoth he, "for the owner's sake.
For if to pluck one single fruit I dare,
These my viziers will lay the garden bare."

BISMARCK SOLILOQUIZES

THE German Emperor—that's his title—not
The one that (thanks to me) his Grandsire got—
Emperor of Germany served his father's turn;
'T will not serve his. Well, well, we live and learn.
I, in my age, have learned one certain thing:
Who makes a king shall perish by a king.

What else should come of making kings? The best
Is but a Policy in purple drest.
I hatched this Policy within my brain:
But shall it hatch a Policy again?
I made an Emperor; made his heir, and he
Has made an Emperor to make mock of me.

Is this the way God laughs at men? to spoil
Their work, and bring to nothingness their toil?
To give the seed, the wit to make it grow,
Patience to nurse this tree till blossoms blow,

ROWEN

To lend the fatness of the labored land,
And turn the fruit to dust within the hand?
If so — His ways shall not be understood —
Let me laugh, too. Surely the jest is good
I have time for laughing now. In days gone by
We had no laughing-times, my kings and I:
Nor did I dream such gratitude was theirs
To save my latter years from statecraft's cares,
And let me sit in calm retirement down
To watch a youthful Emperor play the clown!

Right well you play it, William mine — how well,
It takes a critic old as I to tell.
No madder jest a merry mind could plan
Than Kings coquetting with the Laboring Man.
A gay conceit, indeed, it seems to me —
That Congress, summoned by your high decree
To view the woes of man, and find a cure
For you to guarantee as swift and sure.
Nor did your humor miss a happy chance
When you dispatched your Mother into France.
Of course, to give the joke its subtle sting,
A Grandmother would be the proper thing.
Still, 't was amusing — and instructive, since
It shows just what can make a Frenchman wince,

ROWEN

Make his lip quiver and his thin cheek blanch —
A conqueror's widow with an olive branch.
Oh, had she gone — the jest to carry through —
To see if sparks still lingered at St. Cloud!
Play your game out, boy: I will look and laugh.
Thresh over the poor wheat I threshed to chaff.
Learn the hard lesson I so long have known,
That steel's the only metal for a throne.
You are — your guns, and nothing else on earth,
Except the brutal accident of birth.
Think you the golden years will come again
When the poor peasants, fleeing from the plain,
Huddled beneath the castle walls, stretched hands
To pray the War Lord to protect their lands
Against the alien plunderer, kissed the sod,
And thought him regent of Almighty God?
Why, child, that dogma of your heaven-sent right
Is, in this day, a mere excuse polite
For owning cannon; and the more you own
The more divine your right is to the throne.
Think you these people whose intelligence
Fills you with proud paternal confidence
Have learned — you let them learn — to write and read,
To find out ways of bettering their breed —
Yet hold themselves still made for you to bleed?

ROWEN

And does the spider educate the fly,
Teaching him: "By this belly know that I
Can chain you; this my glittering web is set
To hold your feet fast in a sticky net.
So, now, walk in, I pray. Divinest Right
Has given me a pretty appetite!"
Madman and babe — you send your fly to school;
And then expect your fly to be your fool!

Play on, play on! *I* kept your "right" alive;
I made a medieval dogma thrive
On barren modern soil; but *my* War Lord
In one hand bore a whip; in one a sword.
His Right men held Divine; his title clear—
Through gratitude? through love? — hope? —
                      Fool! through Fear!

IMITATION

MY love she leans from the window
    Afar in a rosy land;
And red as a rose are her blushes,
    And white as a rose her hand.

And the roses cluster around her,
    And mimic her tender grace;
And nothing but roses can blossom
    Wherever she shows her face.

I dwell in a land of winter,
    From my love a world apart —
But the snow blooms over with roses
    At the thought of her in my heart.

* * * * *

This German style of poem
    Is uncommonly popular now;
For the worst of us poets can do it —
    Since Heine showed us how.

"MAGDALENA"

SAT we 'neath the dark verandah,
    Years and years ago;
And I softly pressed a hand a
    Deal more white than snow.
And I cast aside my *reina*,
    As I gazed upon her face,
And I read her "Magdalena,"
    While she smoothed her Spanish lace —
Read her Waller's "Magdalena"—
    She had Magdalena's grace.
Read her of the Spanish duel,
Of the brother, courtly, cruel,
Who between the British wooer
    And the Seville lady came;
How her lover promptly slew her
    Brother, and then fled in shame —
How he dreamed, in long years after,
Of the river's rippling laughter —

ROWEN

    Of the love he used to know
In the myrtle-curtained villa
Near the city of Sevilla
    Years and years ago.

Ah, how warmly was I reading,
    As I gazed upon her face!
And my voice took tones of pleading,
    For I sought to win her grace.
Surely, thought I, in her veins
Runs some drop of foreign strains —
There is something half Castilian
In that lip that shames vermilion;
In that mass of raven tresses,
Tossing like a falcon's jesses;
In that eye with trailing lashes,
And its witching upward flashes —
    Such, indeed, I know,
Shone where Guadalquivir plashes
    Years and years ago.

Looking in her face I read it —
    How the metre trips! —
And the god of lovers sped it
    On my happy lips —

ROWEN

All those words of mystic sweetness
Spoke I with an airy neatness,
As I never had before —
As I cannot speak them more —
Reja, plaza, and mantilla,
"No palabras" and Sevilla,
Caballero and sombrero,
And duenna' and Duero,
Spada, señor, sabe Dios —
Smooth as pipe of Melibœus —
Ah, how very well I read it,
    Looking in her lovely eyes!
When 't was o'er, I looked for credit,
    As she softly moved to rise.

  *   *   *   *   *

Doting dream, ah, dream fallacious —
    Years and years ago! —
For she only said: "My gracious —
    What a lot of French you know!"

MAY the light of some morning skies
    In days when the sun knew how to rise,
Stay with my spirit until I go
To be the boy that I used to know.

"ONE, TWO, THREE!"

IT was an old, old, old, old lady,
    And a boy that was half-past three;
And the way that they played together
    Was beautiful to see.

She could n't go running and jumping,
    And the boy, no more could he;
For he was a thin little fellow,
    With a thin little twisted knee.

They sat in the yellow sunlight,
    Out under the maple-tree;
And the game that they played I 'll tell you,
    Just as it was told to me.

It was Hide-and-Go-Seek they were playing,
    Though you 'd never have known it to be —
With an old, old, old, old lady,
    And a boy with a twisted knee.

ROWEN

The boy would bend his face down
    On his one little sound right knee,
And he 'd guess where she was hiding,
    In guesses One, Two, Three!

"You are in the china-closet!"
    He would cry, and laugh with glee —
It was n't the china-closet;
    But he still had Two and Three.

"You are up in Papa's big bedroom,
    In the chest with the queer old key!"
And she said: "You are *warm* and *warmer;*
    But you 're not quite right," said she.

"It can't be the little cupboard
    Where Mama's things used to be —
So it must be the clothes-press, Gran'ma!"
    And he found her with his Three.

Then she covered her face with her fingers,
    That were wrinkled and white and wee,
And she guessed where the boy was hiding,
    With a One and a Two and a Three.

ROWEN

And they never had stirred from their places,
>   Right under the maple-tree —
This old, old, old, old lady,
>   And the boy with the lame little knee —
This dear, dear, dear old lady,
>   And the boy who was half-past three.

THE LITTLE SHOP

Air: The Bailiff's Daughter of Islington

I KNOW a shop, and a funny little shop,
    In a street that lies anigh;
And I saw the sign set on the door,
    One day as I went by.
And oh! it was so poor and small
    I could not help but stop,
As you would stop, if you should come
    On such a little shop.

I went inside, and found a little boy,
    Far older, I am sure, than I;
He said to me: "Kind sir, what toy
    Will you kindly be pleased to buy?"
And I bought a horse that was painted so red
    As never was charger yet;
One penny, one penny was all I paid
    That splendid horse to get.

ROWEN

For pity of them that were so poor
    I bought me a host of things:
A Noah's Ark without a roof;
    A dove without its wings;
A little trumpet made of tin,
    That cost a single cent —
And all the time that little boy
    Knew just how my money went.

He was, oh! so old, this funny little boy,
    And so sober and so kind:
He sold a five-cent doll for three,
    Because one eye was blind.
And, oh! how proud he was to sell
    Each poor and petty toy,
For he was left to keep the shop,
    This poor little old-time boy.

There is a babe, and a well-beloved babe,
    A babe that belongs to me;
I brought her home these penny toys
    To deck her Christmas tree.
And on that Christmas tree there hung
    A world of trifles fair,
For all the folk that love her well
    Had set their kindness there.

ROWEN

But of all the toys, of all the many toys,
    Was naught that pleased her mind
Except the trumpet made of tin,
    And the doll with one eye blind.
And best of all that Christmas brought,
    She held one little toy
That I bought for a cent in the little shop,
    To please that aged boy.

GRANDFATHER WATTS'S PRIVATE FOURTH

GRANDFATHER WATTS used to tell us boys
That a Fourth wa'n't a Fourth without any noise.
He would say, with a thump of his hickory stick,
That it made an American right down *sick*
To see his sons on the Nation's Day
Sit round, in a sort of a listless way,
With no oration and no train-band,
No fire-work show and no root-beer stand;
While his grandsons, before they were out of bibs,
Were ashamed — Great Scott! — to fire off squibs.

And so, each Independence morn,
Grandfather Watts took his powder-horn,
And the flint-lock shot-gun *his* father had
When he fought under Schuyler, a country lad;

ROWEN

And Grandfather Watts would start and tramp
Ten miles to the woods at Beaver Camp;
For Grandfather Watts used to say — and scowl —
That a decent chipmunk, or woodchuck, or owl
Was better company, friendly or shy,
Than folks who did n't keep Fourth of July.
And so he would pull his hat down on his brow,
And march for the woods, sou'-east by sou'.

But once — ah, long, long years ago, —
For Grandfather 's gone where good men go, —
One hot, hot Fourth, by ways of our own
(Such short-cuts as boys have always known),
We hurried, and followed the dear old man
Beyond where the wilderness began —
To the deep black woods at the foot of the Hump;
And there was a clearing — and a stump.

A stump in the heart of a great wide wood,
And there on that stump our Grandfather stood,
Talking and shouting out there in the sun,
And firing that funny old flint-lock gun
Once in a minute — his head all bare —
Having his Fourth of July out there:
The Fourth of July that he used to know,
Back in eighteen-and-twenty or so!

ROWEN

First, with his face to the heavens blue,
He read the "Declaration" through;
And then, with gestures to left and right,
He made an oration erudite,
Full of words six syllables long —
And then our Grandfather burst into song!
And, scaring the squirrels in the trees,
Gave "Hail, Columbia!" to the breeze.

And I tell you the old man never heard
When we joined in the chorus, word for word!
But he sang out strong to the bright blue sky;
And if voices joined in his Fourth of July,
He heard them as echoes from days gone by.

And when he had done, we all slipped back,
As still as we came, on our twisting track,
While words more clear than the flint-lock shots
Rang in our ears.   And Grandfather Watts?

He shouldered the gun his father bore,
And marched off home, nor'-west by nor'.

TO MY DAUGHTER

CONCERNING A BUNCH OF BLOSSOMS

THE blossoms she gave him — indeed, they were fair;
And grateful the odor they cast on the air;
And he put them in water, and set them anigh
His little round window that looked on the sky.
And the blush of those blossoms, their pleasant perfume,
Made a sweet little spot in that dull little room —
Made a sweet little spot for a day and an hour;
Then —
        Well, little Lil, what 's the fate of a flower?

The blossoms she gave him — indeed, they were fair;
But I think that the least of the giving was there,
In that vase by the window — the look in her face —
Her tender and youthful and delicate grace —

ROWEN

The voice that just trembled in gentle replies,
The look and the light in her uplifted eyes —
Ah! these to my thinking were dearer by far
Than ever the fairest of May-blossoms are.

The blossoms she gave him — you ask, little Lil,
With a lip that is quivering and blue eyes that fill —
If they faded?
          They did — but there's no need to cry!
For they blossomed again where I can't have them die —
These roseate tints on your soft little cheek,
In a manner mysterious certainly speak
Of a bunch of pink blossoms, fresh torn from the tree,
That in eighteen-and-eighty your mother gave me.

SCHUBERT'S KINDER-SCENEN

THE spirit of the Ingle Nook
    Has come to lead me forth,
To wonder at the leaping brook —
    The wind from out the north.

To wander with Haroun the Great
    Through groves of Eastern scent;
To watch beyond the garden gate
    The birds fly, heavenward bent;

To lie amid the grass, and dream
    Each slim and spreading spire
A tufted palm, lit by the gleam
    Of distant heavens' fire.

To dream and dream of things beyond
    The gate — beyond to-day —
Until upon the miller's pond
    The low red light shall play.

ROWEN

And then, when all my dreams shall swim
    To murmuring of the brook,
I shall be led from twilight dim
    Back to the Ingle Nook.

www.ingramcontent.com/pod-product-compliance
Lightning Source LLC
Chambersburg PA
CBHW031409160426
43196CB00007B/952